EUROPE

ASIA

PACIFIC OCEAN

AFRICA

INDIAN OCEAN

OCEANIA

ANTARCTICA

Titles in this series
Animal Alphabet Book
Birds
Plants
Animals
Animal Homes

The publishers would like to thank the staff of World Wildlife Fund
for their help in making these books.

Acknowledgment:
Front and back cover and endpaper illustrations by Stephen Lings.

LADYBIRD BOOKS, INC.
Auburn, Maine 04210 U.S.A.
© LADYBIRD BOOKS LTD 1988
Loughborough, Leicestershire, England
Panda logo © 1986 Copyright WWF – International

Printed in England

WORLD WILDLIFE FUND

Birds

written by GILLIAN DORFMAN
illustrated by PHIL WEARE

Ladybird Books

Produced in association with World Wildlife Fund

Look! What do you see?
Birds – many kinds of birds.

hummingbird

albatross

macaw

penguin

ostrich

All birds are animals. Do you know what makes birds different from other animals?

owl

toucan

kingfisher

quetzal

grebe

flamingo

Birds lay eggs. But so do other animals!

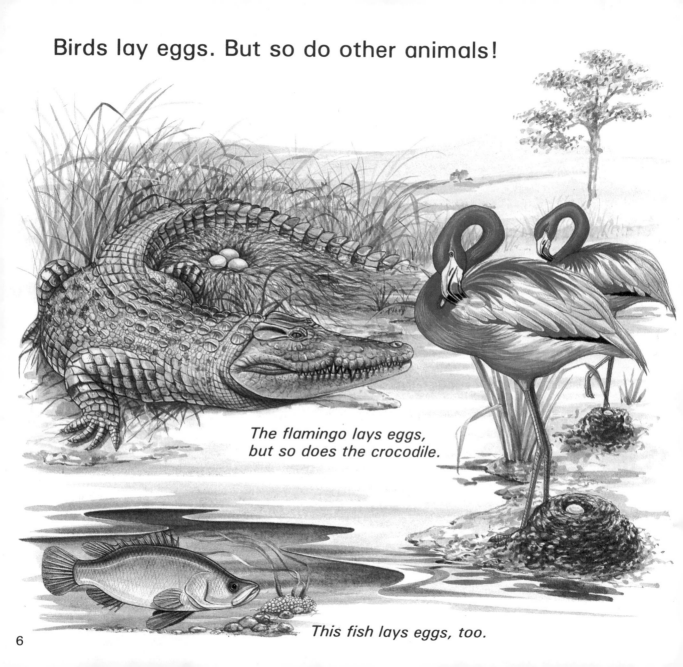

The flamingo lays eggs,
but so does the crocodile.

This fish lays eggs, too.

Birds have wings. But so do other animals!
So what makes birds special?

The owl has wings,
but so does the moth.

Bats have
wings, too.

It's their feathers! Birds are covered with feathers. No other animal has them. So it's their feathers that make birds special.

Big feathers on their wings help these swans fly.

These ducks are cleaning and oiling their feathers. This is called preening.

This goose is shedding
its feathers.
It is molting.

Small feathers on their bodies
help keep these ducks warm.

9

Most birds can fly. Their wings help them fly. Small birds flap their wings quickly, but big birds flap their wings slowly.

house martin

sand martin

kingfisher

heron

pelican

Sometimes birds can fly without flapping.
This bird can fly for a long time without
flapping its wings at all.

The albatross has long, thin wings.
Ocean winds lift the bird and
it soars in the air.

This is an ostrich. It doesn't fly.
But it can run fast enough to escape from danger,
and it can give a nasty kick!

This is a penguin. It doesn't fly either.
But its wings help it swim
as well as a fish can.

These birds are eating. They use their beaks
to get their food. Every beak has
a special shape to do its job well.

The hummingbird's beak is long
and thin, so it can sip
sweet juice from inside flowers.

The heron's beak is like a spear.
It can stab fish.

The woodpecker's beak is
like a chisel. It can tap holes
in trees to get at the insects
that live inside.

These birds use their beaks and feet to help them eat.

The eagle has a sharp, pointed beak for eating its prey, which it catches and grips with its claws.

The parrot has a strong beak for breaking open nuts and fruit. It holds the food tightly with its toes as it eats.

What are these birds doing?

Ducks swim, using their
webbed feet as paddles.

The heron wades.
Its long toes keep it
from sinking into the soft mud.

The shape of their feet helps them do these things well.

The woodpecker searches for food. Its toes help it cling to the tree trunk.

The chaffinch sleeps.
Its toes lock around the branch
to keep it from falling off its perch.

These brightly colored birds are showing off their fine feathers. One of them dances to attract a mate.

A plain brown female bird watches this male cock-of-the-rock dance.

This bird is singing. He sings to attract a mate and to defend his home. Or maybe he sings because he is happy — he has found a mate!

The male nightingale's feathers may be dull, but his song is beautiful.

Most birds build nests to keep their eggs and young safe and warm. Some birds build them in high places...

These gulls bring grass to build their nest high on a cliff ledge.

...and some build them in low places.

The duck plucks its own feathers to line its nest.

Some birds build nests in trees, and others build them on water.

The woodpecker drills a hole in a tree trunk and builds its nest inside.

The thrush shapes its nest, which looks like a cup.

The grebe builds a nest that floats on water.

Mother birds lay eggs in the nests. Baby birds grow inside the eggs.

There are two baby gulls growing inside these eggs.

Four baby thrushes are growing inside these eggs.

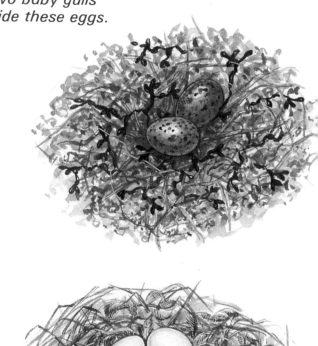

There are ten baby ducks growing inside these eggs.

If the eggs get cold the baby birds inside them will die, so the mother bird, or sometimes the father bird, sits on the eggs and keeps them warm until the baby birds are ready to come out.

This male thrush brings food to the female, who is sitting on her eggs.

When these baby thrushes are born they have no feathers, and they cannot see. But they soon grow feathers, and their eyes open. They are always hungry.

The parents of these baby thrushes find food for their young, and keep them safe and warm.

When these ducklings are born they have fuzzy feathers, and they can see. They are not helpless. They can run and find food.

These ducklings are following their mother into the water.

As young birds grow up they learn to fly.
Some learn quickly...

Young swallows fly well the first time they try.

...and others need to try again and again!

Young sparrows soon learn to fly just as well as their parents.

When these young birds grow up, they will find mates and have young of their own.

Like all birds, they will need safe places to find their food, build their nests, and lay their eggs. Then we can all enjoy watching them as they share the world with us.

WWF

Many of our world's plants and animals
are in danger. People have destroyed or polluted the
places in which they live or grow. Some animals
have been hunted until every one of them has been
killed. This is what happened to the dodo, an
amazing flightless bird that once lived in Mauritius.
The same thing could happen to gorillas, tigers, and
whales unless we do something to save them now.

WWF (World Wildlife Fund) was set up to warn people
about the dangers threatening the earth's wildlife.
If we know and care about what happens to
our world, we may be able to protect it
before too much damage is done.

World Wildlife Fund
Membership Dept. LB89
1250 24th Street N.W.
Washington, D.C. 20037

DATE DUE

JAN 22 '09	